P9-DDD-989

EFFORTLESS CHILLED DESSERTS
THAT EVERYONE WILL LOVE

Olivia Mack McCool

NEW YORK

Text by Olivia Mack McCool
Photographs by Scott Gordon Bleicher

Published by Dovetail in New York, NY.
Dovetail is the publishing imprint of W&P, a division of Very Great Inc.

For details or ordering information, contact the publisher at the address below or email info@dovetail.press.

Dovetail
52 Mercer Street, 3rd Floor
New York, NY 10013
www.dovetail.press

Library of Congress Cataloging-in-Publication data is on file with the publisher.

ISBN: 978-1-73269-521-4

First printing, April 2019

Printed in China

10 9 8 7 6 5 4 3 2

Contents

INTRODUCTION 8

FLAVORED ICE CUBES 10

FLAVORED CHOCOLATES 16

CHOCOLATE TRUFFLES 24

JELLIES 30

FROYO POPS 40

ICE POPS 48

CHEESECAKE BITES 56

PANNA COTTA 64

ICE CREAM SANDWICHES 72

CRISPY RICE TREATS 82

INDEX 90

ABOUT THE AUTHOR 96

Introduction

A silicone ice tray is a useful kitchen item for a number of reasons beyond just making perfectly shaped ice. Spend a few minutes on the internet and you'll find plenty of blog posts and videos demonstrating the creative—and easy—culinary uses of an ice tray: infused ice cubes, frozen flavor bombs of sauces and herbs, and lots of inventive dessert concoctions. As long as you have a high-quality ice tray made of silicone, anything is possible!

Desserts seem to be the perfect second act for your ice trays. They are the simplest, most foolproof vessels for making an infinite number of customizable no-bake sweets—just pour or layer your ingredients into them and pop them in the freezer or fridge. This is a great tactic for days when you're entertaining on short notice, need a lot of individually portioned desserts in a snap, or when you want to involve the kids in a fun hands-on kitchen activity. The silicone ice trays are nonstick and flexible, which makes serving the desserts a breeze; the contents pop out of the molds easily, intact, and in perfectly preportioned sizes.

This book is a collection of just such easy no-bake dessert recipes, to have in your arsenal for when you don't feel like baking or don't want to turn your oven on in the summer. Make things like mini cheesecakes (page 56), which can be served as a sweet ending to any dinner party; chocolate truffles (page 24), perfect for year-round homemade gifts and bake-sales; ice cream sandwiches (page 72) that will impress little guests at birthday parties (sprinkles included!); and even panna cotta (page 64), an Italian custard dessert fit for the toughest dessert critic in your family.

The recipes in this book call for two sizes of ice trays: trays with standard-size cubes, which produce cubes with approximately 1¼-inch sides, and larger-cube trays, which produce ice cubes with approximately 2¼-inch sides. The standard trays are used in most recipes to make perfect bite-sized desserts. The larger cube trays are used primarily in the panna cotta recipes, but are suitable for any treat, as all the recipes in this book have been designed for easy scalability.

Flavored Ice Cubes

Although these are the simplest cubes to make, they deliver a definite wow factor. Flavored ice cubes are a visually enticing way to spruce up even a simple glass of sparkling water or iced tea. They're also a great way to create slow-melting flavor waves in your coffee or matcha drink.

Matcha Latte Cubes

Use these cubes to make the perfect matcha beverage. Just add almond milk and let them slowly release the goodness of matcha tea as they melt. This trendy Japanese green tea has a more calming release of caffeine than coffee, so it's a perfect morning beverage for those who don't like to overcaffeinate.

MAKES 12 ICE CUBES

1¾ CUPS ALMOND MILK

1 TABLESPOON MATCHA

1 TABLESPOON HONEY OR PURE MAPLE SYRUP

In a small bowl, whisk all the ingredients together until there are no lumps. Pour the mixture through a fine-mesh sieve into a measuring cup or other vessel with a spout. Pour the mixture into a silicone ice tray, dividing evenly among 12 cubes. Place in the freezer until frozen solid.

Iced Coffee Cubes

Use these cubes in your iced coffee to double up on the flavor, or make a delicious latte by splashing your preferred milk over the top.

MAKES 12 ICE CUBES

1¾ CUPS ICED COFFEE

Pour the iced coffee into a silicone ice tray, dividing evenly among 12 cubes. Place in the freezer until frozen solid.

Lemon Ice Cubes

Very few beverages can compete with a crisp, cold seltzer with a hint of lemon. This ice cube is a shortcut that infuses the lemon right into the ice cube. Feel free to use up any leftover lemon halves in the fridge.

MAKES 12 ICE CUBES

⅓ CUP LEMON JUICE
12 SMALL LEMON WEDGES

Pour the lemon juice into a silicone ice tray, dividing evenly among 12 cubes. Place a lemon wedge in each cube and cover with water. Place in the freezer until frozen solid.

Mint Ice Cubes

An ice cube packed with fresh mint instantly upgrades any iced or sweet tea. Plus, it adds great visual appeal. Use the old bartender trick of gently smacking the mint sprigs against your hand before plucking and placing them in the ice tray; this helps get the most flavor from the herb.

MAKES 12 ICE CUBES

12 MINT LEAVES

Divide the mint leaves among 12 cubes of a silicone ice tray and cover with water. Place in the freezer until frozen solid.

Matcha Latte Cubes

Lemon Ice Cubes

Iced Coffee Cubes

Mint Ice Cubes

Flavored Chocolates

Prepare to be amazed at your talents as a chocolatier. The treats in this chapter are made by pouring melted chocolate into your ice tray and sprinkling each piece with a variety of toppings. Try any chocolate-fruit-nut combo you can think of. You can store them in the fridge or freezer for weeks—just make sure to allow them to come to room temperature before serving.

Spiced Mexican Chocolates

This sweet-and-spicy combo might not be the first thing that comes to mind when you think about chocolate, but the flavor pairing is a beloved Mexican tradition for a reason. The cinnamon and cayenne give both dark and milk chocolate a pleasant kick. You'll also find that flavoring chocolate with spices is a breeze—simply melt it and stir in the desired spices.

MAKES 12 CHOCOLATES

6 OUNCES	DARK OR MILK CHOCOLATE, CHOPPED
½ TEASPOON	CINNAMON
¼ TEASPOON	CAYENNE
2 TABLESPOONS	ROASTED SALTED PEANUTS, FINELY CHOPPED

Place the chocolate in a heatproof bowl and set over a small pot of simmering water, making sure the bottom of the bowl does not touch the water. Melt the chocolate, stirring occasionally.

Remove from the heat and stir in the cinnamon and cayenne. Alternatively, you can microwave the chocolate in 10-second intervals, stirring in between, until the chocolate has melted.

Pour the melted chocolate into a silicone ice tray, dividing evenly among 12 cubes. Sprinkle with the peanuts and transfer to the refrigerator or freezer to chill for at least 2 hours.

Fruit and Nut Chocolates

The trinity of chocolate, nuts, and fruit is hard to beat, and this recipe shows why. Loaded with raisins, salty pistachios, and cashews, these chocolates are the perfect late afternoon snack. They also make a great homemade holiday gift for friends and family.

MAKES 12 CHOCOLATES

6 OUNCES DARK OR MILK CHOCOLATE, CHOPPED

⅓ CUP PISTACHIOS, CASHEWS, OR ANY OTHER COMBINATION OF NUTS, CHOPPED

⅓ CUP DRIED RAISINS, CRANBERRIES, OR ANY OTHER COMBINATION OF DRIED FRUIT, CHOPPED

Place the chocolate in a heatproof bowl and set over a small pot of simmering water, making sure the bottom of the bowl does not touch the water. Melt the chocolate, stirring occasionally. Alternatively, you can microwave the chocolate in 10-second intervals, stirring in between, until the chocolate has melted.

Pour the melted chocolate into a silicone ice tray, dividing evenly among 12 cubes. Sprinkle with the chopped nuts and dried fruit and transfer to the refrigerator or freezer to chill for at least 2 hours.

Tahini Swirl Chocolates
Fruit and Nut Chocolates

Tahini Swirl Chocolates

Tahini, a paste made of ground sesame seeds often used in Mediterranean cuisine, is the perfect partner for chocolate. The creaminess of the tahini enriches the chocolate and balances its sweetness, reminiscent of the peanut butter and chocolate combo.

MAKES 12 CHOCOLATES

6 OUNCES	DARK OR MILK CHOCOLATE, CHOPPED
2 TABLESPOONS	TAHINI
1 TABLESPOON	TOASTED SESAME SEEDS
PINCH OF	FLAKY SEA SALT

Place the chocolate in a heatproof bowl and set over a small pot of simmering water, making sure the bottom of the bowl does not touch the water. Melt the chocolate, stirring occasionally. Alternatively, you can microwave the chocolate in 10-second intervals, stirring in between, until the chocolate has melted.

Remove from the heat and add the tahini to the chocolate. Stir once to just swirl the tahini.

Pour the melted chocolate into a silicone ice tray, dividing evenly among 12 cubes. Sprinkle with the sesame seeds and flaky sea salt, and transfer to the refrigerator or freezer to chill for at least 2 hours.

Orange and Hazelnut Chocolates

Adding the zest of various citrus fruits is another great way to add flavor to chocolate. The essential oils in the zest will impart a fresh and fruity aroma. Toast the hazelnuts in a dry pan for five minutes if you want a stronger, nuttier flavor.

MAKES 12 CHOCOLATES

6 OUNCES	DARK OR MILK CHOCOLATE, CHOPPED
ZEST OF	1 ORANGE
⅓ CUP	HAZELNUTS, CHOPPED

Place the chocolate in a heatproof bowl and set over a small pot of simmering water, making sure the bottom of the bowl does not touch the water. Melt the chocolate, stirring occasionally.

Remove from the heat and stir in the orange zest. Alternatively, you can microwave the chocolate in 10-second intervals, stirring in between, until the chocolate has melted.

Pour the melted chocolate into a silicone ice tray, dividing evenly among 12 cubes. Sprinkle with the hazelnuts and transfer to the refrigerator or freezer to chill for at least 2 hours.

White Chocolates with Macadamia Nuts and Coconut

White chocolate is usually looked down on by chocolate savants for being too sweet. Use this recipe to change their minds! The addition of lime zest, shredded coconut, and chopped macadamia nuts gives these white chocolates a floral and almost tropical flavor that even the biggest chocolate snobs will enjoy. If you're unable to find white chocolate bars, subbing in chips will do just fine.

MAKES 12 CHOCOLATES

6 OUNCES	WHITE CHOCOLATE, CHOPPED, OR 1 CUP WHITE CHOCOLATE CHIPS
ZEST OF	1 LIME
⅓ CUP	MACADAMIA NUTS, CHOPPED
⅓ CUP	TOASTED SHREDDED COCONUT

Place the white chocolate in a heatproof bowl and set over a small pot of simmering water, making sure the bottom of the bowl does not touch the water. Melt the white chocolate, stirring occasionally.

Remove from the heat and stir in the lime zest. Alternatively, you can microwave the chocolate in 10-second intervals, stirring in between, until the chocolate has melted.

Pour the melted white chocolate into a silicone ice tray, dividing evenly among 12 cubes. Sprinkle with the macadamia nuts and coconut and transfer to the refrigerator or freezer to chill for at least 2 hours.

Chocolate Truffles

The word *truffles* can conjure up images of complicated recipes and kitchen disasters. But these treats are nothing more than layers of melted chocolate and easy-to-make fillings. The silicone of the ice tray creates the perfect nonstick mold, so you never have to worry about getting the shape right. The truffles last in the fridge and freezer for weeks, just make sure you allow them to come to room temperature before serving.

Chocolate Coconut Truffles

Why have a processed candy bar when you can make these impressive, no-bake truffles? Using dark chocolate for this recipe is preferred; it cuts the sweetness of the coconut flakes and gives the truffle a nice richness.

MAKES 12 TRUFFLES

¼ CUP	SWEETENED CONDENSED MILK
½ CUP	SWEETENED COCONUT FLAKES
½ TEASPOON	VANILLA EXTRACT
1 CUP	CONFECTIONERS' SUGAR, PLUS MORE AS NEEDED
6 OUNCES	DARK CHOCOLATE, CHOPPED, OR 1 CUP DARK CHOCOLATE CHIPS
2 TABLESPOONS	COCONUT OIL

In a large bowl, combine the sweetened condensed milk, coconut, and vanilla and stir together. Using a rubber spatula, stir in the confectioners' sugar. The mixture should be thick and sticky; add more confectioners' sugar if the mixture is too wet or loose. Set aside.

Combine the chocolate and coconut oil in a heatproof bowl. Place the bowl over a small pot of simmering water, making sure the bottom of the bowl does not touch the water. Melt the chocolate, stirring occasionally. Remove from the heat. Alternatively, you can microwave the chocolate in 10-second intervals, stirring in between, until the chocolate has melted.

Spoon two-thirds of the melted chocolate into a silicone ice tray, dividing evenly among 12 cubes (about 2 teaspoons in each cube). Tilt the tray so that the chocolate coats all 4 sides of each cube. Repeat 3 or 4 times to ensure there's an even layer. Transfer to the freezer immediately and chill for 10 minutes. Reserve the remaining chocolate in the same bowl.

Remove the ice tray from the freezer. Dust your hands with confectioners' sugar and make a grape-size ball (1 heaping teaspoon) from the coconut filling. Place the ball in a chocolate-coated cube and press down on it with your fingers. Repeat the process for the remaining cubes.

Spoon the remaining chocolate on top of the coconut filling, dispersing evenly. Transfer to the freezer for another 30 minutes until completely solid.

Store in the refrigerator until ready to serve.

Chocolate Peppermint Truffles

This is a homemade version of the iconic peppermint patty. The beloved holiday treat is re-created with only five ingredients, and making it at home means you know exactly what's in it. Look for peppermint extract in the baking aisle of most supermarkets.

MAKES 12 TRUFFLES

⅓ CUP	SWEETENED CONDENSED MILK
1 TEASPOON	PEPPERMINT EXTRACT
1½ CUPS	CONFECTIONERS' SUGAR, PLUS MORE AS NEEDED
6 OUNCES	DARK CHOCOLATE, CHOPPED, OR 1 CUP DARK CHOCOLATE CHIPS
2 TABLESPOONS	COCONUT OIL

In a large bowl, combine the sweetened condensed milk and peppermint extract and stir together. Using a rubber spatula, stir in the confectioners' sugar. The mixture should be thick and sticky; add more confectioners' sugar if the mixture is too wet or loose. Set aside.

Combine the chocolate and coconut oil in a heat-proof bowl. Place the bowl over a small pot of simmering water, making sure the bottom of the bowl does not touch the water. Melt the chocolate, stirring occasionally. Remove from the heat.

Alternatively, you can microwave the chocolate in 10-second intervals, stirring in between, until the chocolate has melted.

Spoon two-thirds of the melted chocolate into a silicone ice tray, dividing evenly among 12 cubes (about 2 teaspoons in each cube). Tilt the tray so that the chocolate coats all 4 sides of each cube. Repeat 3 or 4 times to ensure there's an even layer. Transfer to the freezer immediately and chill for 10 minutes. Reserve the remaining chocolate in the same bowl.

Remove the ice tray from the freezer. Dust your hands with confectioners' sugar and make a grape-size ball (1 heaping teaspoon) from the peppermint filling. Place the ball in a chocolate-coated cube and press down on it with your fingers. Repeat the process for the remaining cubes.

Spoon the remaining chocolate on top of the peppermint filling, dispersing evenly. Transfer to the freezer for another 30 minutes until completely solid.

Store in the refrigerator until ready to serve.

Chocolate, Peanut Butter, and Pretzel Truffles

Chocolate and peanut butter is well established as a seriously delicious combo. However, adding pretzels takes things to a whole other sweet and salty level. Feel free to use pretzel pieces from the bottom of the pretzel bag; or break pretzels down quickly by giving them a spin in the food processor.

MAKES 12 TRUFFLES

6 OUNCES	DARK CHOCOLATE, CHOPPED, OR 1 CUP DARK CHOCOLATE CHIPS
2 TABLESPOONS	COCONUT OIL
⅓ CUP	SMOOTH PEANUT BUTTER
1 TABLESPOON	CONFECTIONERS' SUGAR
½ CUP	FINELY CRUSHED PRETZELS

In a heatproof bowl, combine the chocolate and coconut oil. Place the bowl over a small pot of simmering water, making sure the bottom of the bowl does not touch the water. Melt the chocolate, stirring occasionally. Remove from the heat. Alternatively, you can microwave the chocolate in 10-second intervals, stirring in between, until the chocolate has melted.

Spoon two-thirds of the melted chocolate into a silicone ice tray, dividing evenly among 12 cubes (about 2 teaspoons in each cube). Tilt the tray so that the chocolate coats all 4 sides of each cube. Repeat 3 or 4 times to ensure there's an even layer. Transfer to the freezer immediately and chill for 10 minutes. Reserve the remaining chocolate in the same bowl.

Combine the peanut butter and confectioners' sugar in a medium bowl. Using a rubber spatula, stir together until well combined. Add the crushed pretzels and stir again; the mixture should be very thick.

Remove the ice tray from the freezer. Spoon about 1 tablespoon of the filling into each cube and gently press down on it with your fingers. Repeat the process for all the remaining cubes.

Spoon the remaining chocolate on top of the peanut-butter filling, dispersing evenly. Transfer to the freezer for another 30 minutes until completely solid.

Store in the refrigerator until ready to serve.

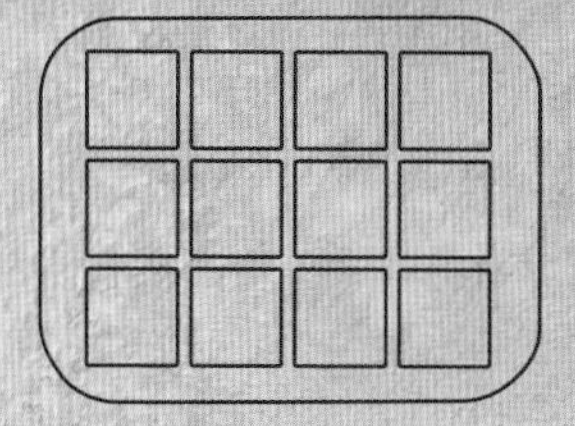

Jellies

Thanks to these inventive yet simple jelly recipes, there's absolutely no need for the artificial-tasting boxed stuff. These refreshing treats have less sugar and more real ingredients, like fruit and herbs, than the commercial alternatives, which means you can feel good about serving these jiggly cubes. For the following recipes, it's important to allow the gelatin to "bloom" by letting it dissolve in liquid. Completing this step ensures that the gelatin dissolves evenly when heated, making for a perfectly smooth and wobbly jelly.

Arnold Palmer Jelly

The Arnold Palmer is a much-loved, classically refreshing drink of our nation. These jellies turn the iced tea and lemonade fusion into a fun, solid form and are a perfect dessert to cap off a light summer lunch.

MAKES 12 JELLY CUBES

1 TABLESPOON	GELATIN
1½ CUPS	LEMONADE, PREFERABLY HOMEMADE
1 TABLESPOON	SUGAR
1	BLACK TEA BAG

In a small bowl, combine the gelatin with ¼ cup of lemonade and let sit.

Meanwhile, in a small saucepan, combine the remaining 1¼ cups of lemonade and the sugar. Bring to a boil, add the tea bag, and turn off the heat. Let the tea steep for 3 minutes. Remove and discard the tea bag.

Add the bloomed gelatin and stir until it has dissolved. Pour the mixture through a fine-mesh sieve into a measuring cup or a vessel with a spout.

Pour the mixture into a silicone ice tray, dividing evenly among 12 cubes. Carefully transfer to the refrigerator and chill for at least 4 hours.

To pop the jelly out of the ice tray, submerge the bottom of the tray in a bowl or dish of hot water for 10 seconds to loosen the cubes.

Store in the refrigerator.

This grown-up take on jelly that even kids will love is a good example of just how easy it is to use fresh herbs to infuse flavor into jellies. Store-bought grapefruit juice works great here, but if you have the time, freshly squeezed juice will take this jelly to the next level.

MAKES 12 JELLY CUBES

1 TABLESPOON	GELATIN
1½ CUPS	GRAPEFRUIT JUICE
2 TABLESPOONS	SUGAR
1 SPRIG	ROSEMARY

In a small bowl, combine the gelatin with ¼ cup of grapefruit juice and let sit.

Meanwhile, in a small saucepan, combine the remaining 1¼ cups of grapefruit juice with the sugar and rosemary sprig. Heat over medium-high heat just until the sugar has dissolved, about 1 to 2 minutes. Turn off the heat and let the mixture steep for 5 minutes, then remove and discard the rosemary sprig.

Add the bloomed gelatin and stir until it has dissolved. Pour the mixture through a fine-mesh sieve into a measuring cup or a vessel with a spout.

Pour the mixture into a silicone ice tray, dividing evenly among 12 cubes.

Carefully transfer to the refrigerator and chill for at least 4 hours.

To pop the jelly out of the ice tray, submerge the bottom of the tray in a bowl or dish of hot water for 10 seconds to loosen the cubes.

Store in the refrigerator.

Piña Colada Jelly

With a flavor that's so classic, these nonalcoholic jelly treats will absolutely impress whomever you're serving them to. Not only are they delicious, but the layers created when the coconut milk separates add a fun visual appeal.

MAKES 12 JELLY CUBES

1 TABLESPOON	GELATIN
1¼ CUPS	PINEAPPLE JUICE
3 TABLESPOONS	SUGAR
½ CUP	CANNED COCONUT MILK

In a small bowl, combine the gelatin with 3 tablespoons of pineapple juice and let sit.

Meanwhile, in a small saucepan, combine the remaining pineapple juice, the sugar, and the coconut milk. Heat over medium-high heat just until steam starts to come off the milk and the sugar has dissolved, about 1 to 2 minutes. Don't let the mixture come to a boil.

Remove from the heat, add the bloomed gelatin, and stir until it has dissolved. Pour the mixture through a fine-mesh sieve into a measuring cup or a vessel with a spout.

Pour the mixture into a silicone ice tray, dividing evenly among 12 cubes. Carefully transfer to the refrigerator and chill for at least 4 hours.

To pop the jelly out of the ice tray, submerge the bottom of the tray in a bowl or dish of hot water for 10 seconds to loosen the cubes.

Store in the refrigerator.

Creamsicle Jelly

This recipe transforms store-bought orange juice and heavy cream, two seemingly boring ingredients, into a dreamy dessert. The touch of vanilla and sugar will create that fruity, creamy flavor that makes everyone nostalgic.

MAKES 12 JELLY CUBES

FOR THE ORANGE LAYER:

2 TEASPOONS	GELATIN
1¼ CUPS	ORANGE JUICE
1 TABLESPOON	SUGAR
¼ TEASPOON	VANILLA EXTRACT

FOR THE CREAM LAYER:

1 TEASPOON	GELATIN
½ CUP	HEAVY CREAM OR HALF-AND-HALF
1 TABLESPOON	SUGAR

Make the orange layer: In a small bowl, combine the gelatin with ¼ cup of orange juice and let sit.

Meanwhile, in a small saucepan, combine the remaining cup of orange juice, the sugar, and the vanilla. Heat over medium-high heat just until the sugar has dissolved, about 1 to 2 minutes.

Remove from the heat and stir in the bloomed gelatin until dissolved. Pour the mixture through a fine-mesh sieve into a measuring cup or a vessel with a spout.

Pour the mixture into a silicone ice tray, dividing evenly among 12 cubes. Carefully transfer to the refrigerator and chill while making the cream layer.

Make the cream layer: In a small bowl, combine the gelatin with 2 tablespoons of cool water and let sit.

Meanwhile, in a small saucepan, combine the heavy cream and sugar. Heat over medium-high heat just until steam starts to come off the milk and the sugar has dissolved, about 1 to 2 minutes. Don't let the mixture come to a boil.

Remove from the heat and stir in the bloomed gelatin until dissolved. Pour the mixture through a fine-mesh sieve into a measuring cup or a vessel with a spout. Let it cool completely.

Pour the cream mixture into the silicone ice tray on top of the orange layer, dividing evenly among 12 cubes. Carefully transfer to the refrigerator and chill for at least 4 hours.

To pop the jelly out of the ice tray, submerge the bottom of the tray in a bowl or dish of hot water for 10 seconds to loosen the cubes.

Store in the refrigerator.

Strawberry Jelly

Made with fresh strawberries, this jelly is a great way to sneak some extra fruit into a delicious treat. The lemon zest provides a nice zip of citrus which keeps this jelly from being too sweet. If you have strawberries that are on the verge of being thrown out, this is the perfect way to use them up.

MAKES 12 JELLY CUBES

1 TABLESPOON	GELATIN
2 CUPS	HULLED AND CHOPPED STRAWBERRIES
ZEST AND JUICE OF	1 LEMON
¼ CUP	SUGAR

In a small bowl, combine the gelatin with ¼ cup of water and let sit for 3 minutes.

Meanwhile, in a blender, puree the strawberries, lemon zest and juice, and sugar until the mixture is very smooth. Transfer the puree to a small saucepan and heat over medium heat until the sugar has dissolved. Remove from the heat, add the bloomed gelatin, and stir until it has dissolved. Pour the mixture through a fine-mesh sieve into a measuring cup or a vessel with a spout.

Pour the mixture into a silicone ice tray, dividing evenly among 12 cubes. Carefully transfer to the refrigerator and chill for at least 4 hours.

To pop the jelly out of the ice tray, submerge the bottom of the tray in a bowl or dish of hot water for 10 seconds to loosen the cubes.

Store in the refrigerator.

Strawberry Jelly

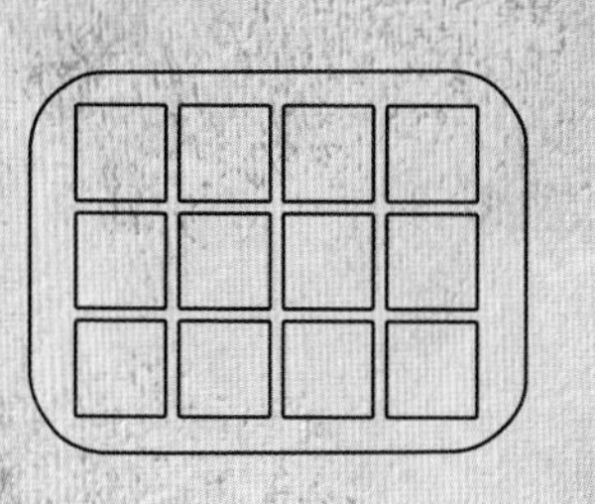

Froyo Pops

Imagine turning your summer breakfast into an ice pop! These mini pops start with a wholesome base of yogurt and feature such mix-ins as pure maple syrup, tahini, and fresh fruit. You can use any kind of yogurt you like, but the higher the fat content, the creamier the pop. It's a guilt-free treat that comes together in a snap.

Breakfast Parfait Pops

These sweet little pops have all the elements of a yogurt parfait and are the perfect make-ahead summer breakfast or year-round snack. Use whatever fruits are in season with different granolas, and you have a recipe you'll want to make again and again.

MAKES 12 POPS

½ CUP	STORE-BOUGHT GRANOLA, LIGHTLY CRUSHED
1 TEASPOON	COCONUT OIL, MELTED
1 CUP	PLAIN YOGURT
1 CUP	MIXED BERRIES (CHOPPED STRAWBERRIES, RASPBERRIES, BLUEBERRIES, OR A COMBINATION)
1 TABLESPOON	PURE MAPLE SYRUP OR HONEY
12	LOLLIPOP STICKS

In a small bowl, stir together the granola and coconut oil. Set aside.

In a medium bowl, combine the yogurt, berries, and maple syrup. Stir until well blended. Transfer to a measuring cup or a vessel with a spout. Pour the mixture into a silicone ice tray, dividing evenly among 12 cubes. Spoon a little of the granola mixture on top of the yogurt in each cube, and, using the back of the spoon, gently press down on the granola. Transfer to the freezer and freeze for 3 hours until the pops are partially frozen.

Insert a lollipop stick in the middle of each cube and return the tray to the freezer. Chill until the pops are completely frozen, about 4 to 5 hours.

Breakfast Parfait Pops

Chocolate and Almond Butter Swirl Froyo Pops

These pops are a little more indulgent than the Breakfast Parfait Pops (page 41), although they still deliver the goodness of plain yogurt, pure maple syrup, and almond butter. When adding the chocolate and almond butter to yogurt, gently stir once or twice to preserve the swirls for a stunning finished product.

MAKES 12 POPS

1 OUNCE	DARK CHOCOLATE, CHOPPED, OR ¼ CUP DARK CHOCOLATE CHIPS
1 TABLESPOON	COCONUT OIL
1½ CUPS	PLAIN YOGURT
1 TABLESPOON	PURE MAPLE SYRUP
2 TABLESPOONS	ALMOND BUTTER
12	LOLLIPOP STICKS

In a heatproof bowl, combine the chocolate and coconut oil. Place the bowl over a small pot of simmering water, making sure the bottom of the bowl does not touch the water. Melt the chocolate, stirring occasionally. Remove from the heat and set aside. Alternatively, you can microwave the chocolate in 10-second intervals, stirring in between, until the chocolate has melted.

In a large measuring cup or a vessel with a spout, mix the yogurt and maple syrup. Add the almond butter and melted chocolate. Using a rubber spatula, swirl the almond butter and chocolate into the yogurt, being careful not to overmix—you want distinctive swirls.

Pour the mixture into a silicone ice tray, dividing evenly among 12 cubes.

Transfer to the freezer and freeze for 3 hours until the pops are partially frozen.

Insert a lollipop stick in the middle of each cube and return the tray to the freezer.

Chill until the pops are completely frozen, about 4 to 5 hours.

Maple and Spice Froyo Pops

This recipe is like Christmas in a popsicle. It uses all of the holiday spices, cinnamon, ginger, and nutmeg, which is why it's totally OK to savor this icy treat in wintertime. If you can, splurge on high-quality maple syrup; it will go a long way to enhance the flavors in this five-ingredient recipe.

MAKES 12 POPS

1½ CUPS	PLAIN YOGURT
¼ CUP	PURE MAPLE SYRUP
½ TEASPOON	CINNAMON
¼ TEASPOON	GROUND FRESH GINGER
⅛ TEASPOON	GROUND NUTMEG
12	LOLLIPOP STICKS

In a medium bowl, combine all the ingredients. Stir until well blended.

Transfer to a measuring cup or a vessel with a spout. Pour the mixture into a silicone ice tray, dividing evenly among 12 cubes. Transfer to the freezer and freeze for 3 hours until the pops are partially frozen. Insert a lollipop stick in the middle of each cube and return the tray to the freezer.

Chill until the pops are completely frozen, about 4 to 5 hours.

Mango Lassi Froyo Pops

A classic Indian drink, mango lassi is a combo of chilled yogurt and fresh mango. No wonder the same ingredients make such a delicious, creamy pop. This version is dressed up with cardamom, and honey adds more sweetness.

MAKES 12 POPS

1 CUP	PLAIN YOGURT
1 CUP	MANGO, PEELED, PITTED, AND DICED OR 1 CUP FROZEN MANGO, THAWED
1 TABLESPOON	HONEY
⅛ TEASPOON	CARDAMOM (OPTIONAL)
12	LOLLIPOP STICKS

Combine all the ingredients in a blender and blend until very smooth.

Transfer to a measuring cup or a vessel with a spout. Pour the mixture into a silicone ice tray, dividing evenly among 12 cubes. Transfer to the freezer and freeze for 3 hours until the pops are partially frozen.

Insert a lollipop stick in the middle of each cube and return the tray to the freezer.

Chill until the pops are completely frozen, about 4 to 5 hours.

Ice Pops

Ice pops are the ultimate canvas for all sorts of fun flavor combinations. The following recipes are jam-packed with ingredients such as chai, fresh peaches, and key limes. These pops are much smaller than a regular popsicle—ideal size for children and adults who don't want to overindulge.

Vietnamese Coffee Ice Pops

Traditional Vietnamese iced coffee is made with sweetened condensed milk, and the end result is a sweet, superrich, creamy drink. Here, all those flavors come together to make incredibly flavorful ice pops. Pouring a second layer of half-and-half on top creates a beautiful visual effect, but if you don't want to wait a few hours to add it, feel free to mix all the ingredients together and pour them into the ice tray all at once.

MAKES 12 ICE POPS

1 CUP	HALF-AND-HALF
½ CUP	SWEETENED CONDENSED MILK
¼ CUP	STRONG COFFEE (OR 1 TEASPOON INSTANT ESPRESSO MIXED WITH ¼ CUP WATER)
¼ TEASPOON	CINNAMON
⅛ TEASPOON	GROUND CARDAMOM
⅛ TEASPOON	VANILLA EXTRACT
12	LOLLIPOP STICKS

In a small bowl, whisk ¼ cup of half-and-half with 2 tablespoons of sweetened condensed milk and set aside.

In a medium bowl, whisk the remaining ¾ cup of half-and-half and ⅜ cup (6 tablespoons) of sweetened condensed milk with the coffee, cinnamon, cardamom, and vanilla until well combined. Pour the mixture into a silicone ice tray, dividing evenly among 12 cubes.

Transfer to the freezer and freeze for 3 hours until the pops are partially frozen. Pour the reserved half-and-half mixture into the ice tray, dividing evenly among 12 cubes. Insert a lollipop stick in the middle of each cube and return the tray to the freezer. Chill until the pops are completely frozen, around 5 hours or overnight.

Peach Raspberry Ice Pops

The combination of fresh peaches and raspberries with just a touch of added sweetness makes for an intensely fruity ice pop. These are best made in the summer, when both peaches and raspberries are at their best.

MAKES 12 ICE POPS

FOR THE PEACH LAYER:

1 CUP	PEELED AND CHOPPED PEACHES (FROM 1 LARGE PEACH) OR 1 CUP FROZEN PEACHES, THAWED
⅓ CUP	WATER
1 TABLESPOON	SUGAR
JUICE AND ZEST OF 1	LIME

FOR THE RASPBERRY LAYER:

½ CUP	RASPBERRIES
2 TABLESPOONS	WATER
1 TABLESPOON	SUGAR
12	LOLLIPOP STICKS

Make the peach layer: Combine all the ingredients in a blender and blend until very smooth.

Pour the mixture into a silicone ice tray, dividing evenly among 12 cubes and leaving room for the raspberry layer.

Transfer to the freezer and freeze for 3 hours until the pops are partially frozen.

Make the raspberry layer: In the same blender (make sure to give it a quick rinse), combine all the ingredients and blend until the mixture is very smooth.

Remove the ice tray from the freezer. Pour the raspberry puree on top of the peach layer, distributing evenly among 12 cubes. Insert a lollipop stick in the middle of each cube and return the tray to the freezer. Chill until the pops are completely frozen, around 5 hours, or overnight.

Coconut Chai Tea Ice Pops

Although they're a nondairy treat, these pops don't skimp on creaminess or flavor—as long as you make sure to use full-fat coconut milk. Chai is a fragrant combination of black tea and such spices as cinnamon, cloves, ginger, and cardamom, flavors reminiscent of a trip to a faraway land.

MAKES 12 ICE POPS

1 (14-OUNCE) CAN	FULL-FAT COCONUT MILK
2	CHAI TEA BAGS
2 TABLESPOONS	PURE MAPLE SYRUP OR HONEY
12	LOLLIPOP STICKS

In a small saucepan, bring the coconut milk to a simmer. Add the tea bags and maple syrup, turn off the heat, and let steep for 4 minutes. Remove and discard the tea bags.

Pour the mixture into a silicone ice tray, dividing evenly among 12 cubes. Transfer to the freezer and freeze for 3 hours until the pops are partially frozen.

Insert a lollipop stick in the middle of each cube and return the tray to the freezer. Chill until the pops are completely frozen, around 5 hours, or overnight.

Key Lime Pie Ice Pops

It doesn't get much better than a perfectly rich key lime pie. In these pops, you get the same tart flavor combined with the sweet graham cracker crust. It's great to use actual key limes when you can find them, but regular limes work well, too (and there's a lot less squeezing involved).

MAKES 12 ICE POPS

6 TO 8	KEY LIMES, OR 2 REGULAR LIMES
½ CUP	SWEETENED CONDENSED MILK
1 CUP	HALF-AND-HALF
¼ TEASPOON	VANILLA EXTRACT
PINCH OF	KOSHER SALT
12	LOLLIPOP STICKS
3	GRAHAM CRACKERS, FINELY CRUSHED (½ CUP CRUMBS)

Zest and juice all the limes; you should have about ½ cup of lime juice.

In a medium bowl, whisk together the sweetened condensed milk, half-and-half, lime juice and zest, vanilla, and salt. Pour the mixture into a silicone ice tray, dividing evenly among 12 cubes.

Transfer to the freezer and freeze for 3 hours until the pops are partially frozen.

Insert a lollipop stick in the middle of each cube and return the tray to the freezer. Chill until the pops are completely frozen, around 5 hours, or overnight.

Place the graham cracker crumbs on a plate. When you're ready to eat the ice pops, submerge the bottom of the tray in a bowl or dish of hot water for 10 seconds to loosen them. Pop out the pops and dip the bottoms and the sides in the graham cracker crumbs before serving.

Key Lime Pie
Ice Pops

Cheesecake Bites

How great would it be to have a tray of mini cheesecakes waiting in your freezer for when cravings hit? Or to present each of your dinner guests with individual cheesecake bites for the last course? These no-bake versions firm up in the freezer, then need to sit just 10 minutes at room temperature to ensure maximum creaminess before serving. The best part? They last for several weeks in the freezer. You'll never want to bake another cheesecake again.

Mango and Ginger Cheesecake

The tropical flavor of this cheesecake makes it the perfect snack to savor in a hammock, under a palm tree, or even just at a picnic. Mango and ginger is an underrated combination, and here the ginger from the cookies cuts the sweetness of the mango just enough.

MAKES 12 PIECES

1 TEASPOON	GELATIN
2 TABLESPOONS	COOL WATER
1 CUP	MANGO, PEELED, PITTED, AND DICED OR 1 CUP FROZEN MANGO, THAWED
2 TABLESPOONS	SUGAR
8 OUNCES	CREAM CHEESE, AT ROOM TEMPERATURE
14	GINGERSNAP COOKIES, FINELY CRUSHED (½ CUP CRUMBS)
2 TABLESPOONS	UNSALTED BUTTER, MELTED

In a small bowl, combine the gelatin and water and set aside.

In the bowl of a food processor, combine the mango and sugar. Puree until very smooth; you should have about ¾ cup of puree. Transfer the mango puree to a small saucepan and heat over medium heat until the sugar has completely dissolved. Turn off the heat, stir in the bloomed gelatin, and let sit for 5 minutes to cool slightly.

In the bowl of a stand mixer fitted with the paddle attachment, add the cream cheese and beat until smooth. Add the mango puree and beat until every-thing is well combined.

Spoon the mixture into a silicone ice tray, dividing evenly among 12 cubes and making sure there's ⅛ inch of space left on top for the crust. Transfer to the freezer to chill while you make the crust.

In a small bowl, combine the gingersnap crumbs and melted butter and stir until the mixture resembles wet sand. Spoon a little of the gingersnap crust on top of each cheesecake. Using the back of the spoon, gently press down on the crumb mixture, making sure the surface is covered evenly.

Transfer the ice tray to the freezer and chill for at least 5 hours, or overnight. To serve, pop each cheese-cake bites out of the tray and let them sit for 10 minutes to come to room temperature.

Vanilla and Raspberry Cheesecake

This recipe mirrors the quintessential cheesecake: graham cracker crust, a thick, creamy vanilla layer, and a raspberry topping. The raspberry jam adds a swirl of delicious tartness to the creaminess of the filling—but feel free to try any variety of jam here, you can't go wrong.

MAKES 12 PIECES

1 TEASPOON	GELATIN
2 TABLESPOONS	COOL WATER
½ CAN (7 OUNCES)	SWEETENED CONDENSED MILK
8 OUNCES	CREAM CHEESE, AT ROOM TEMPERATURE
½ TEASPOON	VANILLA EXTRACT
¼ CUP	RASPBERRY JAM
3	GRAHAM CRACKERS, FINELY CRUSHED (½ CUP CRUMBS)
2 TABLESPOONS	UNSALTED BUTTER, MELTED
1 TABLESPOON	SUGAR

In a small bowl, combine the gelatin and water and set aside.

In a small saucepan over medium heat, heat the sweetened condensed milk just until bubbles start to form on the surface (don't let it boil). Turn off the heat, stir in the bloomed gelatin, and let the mixture sit for 5 minutes to cool slightly.

In the bowl of a stand mixer fitted with the paddle attachment, combine the cream cheese and vanilla. Beat until smooth. Add the sweetened condensed milk and beat until everything is well combined.

Spoon the raspberry jam on top of the cheesecake filling and, using a rubber spatula, stir once or twice, taking care not to overmix, so you get a swirled effect.

Spoon the mixture into a silicone ice tray, dividing evenly among 12 cubes and making sure there's ⅛ inch of space left on top for the crust. Transfer to the freezer to chill while you make the graham cracker crust.

In a medium bowl, combine the graham cracker crumbs, melted butter, and sugar. Stir the mixture together until it resembles wet sand. Spoon a little of the graham cracker crust on top of each cheesecake. Using the back of the spoon, gently press the crumbs down, making sure the surface is covered evenly.

Transfer the ice tray to the freezer and chill for at least 5 hours, or overnight. To serve, pop the cheesecake bites out of the tray and let them sit for 10 minutes to come to room temperature.

Goat Cheese and Blueberry Cheesecake

Cheesecake is given a sophisticated treatment in this recipe which calls for a combination of regular cream cheese and goat cheese for a richer flavor. The crust, made from speculoos cookies (spiced shortbread), imparts a cinnamon goodness. Serve these cheesecake bites as the perfect end to a stylish dinner party.

MAKES 12 PIECES

8 OUNCES	CREAM CHEESE, AT ROOM TEMPERATURE
5 OUNCES	FRESH GOAT CHEESE, AT ROOM TEMPERATURE
2 TABLESPOONS	CONFECTIONERS' SUGAR
JUICE AND ZEST OF 1	LEMON
¼ CUP	BLUEBERRY JAM
5	SPECULOOS COOKIES, FINELY CRUSHED (½ CUP CRUMBS)
2 TABLESPOONS	UNSALTED BUTTER, MELTED

In the bowl of a stand mixer fitted with the paddle attachment, add the cream cheese, goat cheese, confectioners' sugar, and lemon juice and zest. Beat until smooth.

Spoon the cream cheese mixture into a silicone ice tray, dividing evenly among 12 cubes. Spoon some of the blueberry jam in each cube and, using a wooden skewer or knife, swirl the two parts together. Make sure there's ⅛ inch of space left on top for the crust.

In a small bowl, combine the speculoos cookie crumbs and melted butter. Stir together until the mixture resembles wet sand. Spoon a little of the cookie crust on top of each cheesecake. Using the back of the spoon, gently press down on the crumb mixture, making sure the surface is covered evenly.

Transfer the ice tray to the freezer and chill for at least 4 hours, or overnight. To serve, pop the cheesecake bites out of the tray and let them sit for 10 minutes to come to room temperature.

Mocha Cheesecake

Make this coffeelicious dessert for an afternoon pick-me-up. Instant espresso powder is widely used in baking recipes to give desserts a bold coffee flavor, and works perfectly with the tartness of the cheesecake.

MAKES 12 PIECES

1 TEASPOON	GELATIN
2 TABLESPOONS	COOL WATER
½ CAN (7 OUNCES)	SWEETENED CONDENSED MILK
2 TEASPOONS	COCOA POWDER
1 TEASPOON	INSTANT ESPRESSO POWDER
8 OUNCES	CREAM CHEESE, AT ROOM TEMPERATURE
10	CHOCOLATE WAFER COOKIES, FINELY CRUSHED (½ CUP CRUMBS)
2 TABLESPOONS	UNSALTED BUTTER, MELTED
1 TABLESPOON	SUGAR

In a small bowl, combine the gelatin and water and set aside.

In a small saucepan, combine the condensed milk, cocoa powder, and espresso powder and heat over medium heat until bubbles start to form on the surface (don't let it boil). Turn off the heat, stir in the bloomed gelatin, and let sit for 5 minutes to cool slightly.

In the bowl of a stand mixer fitted with the paddle attachment, add the cream cheese and beat until smooth. Add the condensed milk mixture and beat until everything is well combined.

Spoon the mixture into a silicone ice tray, dividing evenly among 12 cubes, making sure there's ⅛ inch of space left on top for the crust. Transfer to the freezer to chill while you make the crust.

In a small bowl, combine the chocolate wafer crumbs, melted butter, and sugar. Stir together until the mixture resembles wet sand. Spoon a little of the chocolate wafer crust on top of each cheesecake. Using the back of the spoon, gently press down on the crumb mixture, making sure the surface is covered evenly.

Transfer the ice tray to the freezer and chill for at least 5 hours, or overnight. To serve, pop the cheesecake bites out of the tray and let them sit for 10 minutes to come to room temperature.

Panna Cotta

Translated literally, *panna cotta* means "cooked cream" in Italian, and it's an incredibly simple no-bake dessert. Silicone ice trays are the perfect molds for chilling these delicate treats, because their nonstick surface allows the panna cotta to be removed easily without sacrificing the shape. This recipe calls for ice trays with large cubes which create the ideal-sized servings. Store them in the fridge, covered, for up to 3 days.

Vanilla Panna Cotta

This is the essential panna cotta blueprint recipe, which creates a tasty canvas for all sorts of toppings. Fresh berries are great, as is honey, melted chocolate, or chopped mango. A fresh vanilla bean will impart the purest vanilla flavor in your panna cotta, and it's worth the splurge.

MAKES 4 LARGE CUBES

3 TABLESPOONS	COOL WATER
2½ TEASPOONS	GELATIN
2 CUPS	HALF-AND-HALF (OR 1 CUP WHOLE MILK AND 1 CUP HEAVY CREAM)
½	VANILLA BEAN, SPLIT LENGTHWISE AND SEEDS SCRAPED, OR ½ TEASPOON VANILLA EXTRACT
⅓ CUP	SUGAR
	BERRIES OR HONEY, FOR SERVING

In a small bowl, combine the water and gelatin. Set aside.

Meanwhile, in a small saucepan, combine the half-and-half, vanilla bean and seeds, and sugar. Bring to a simmer, turn off the heat, and let steep for 5 minutes. Remove the vanilla bean.

Add the bloomed gelatin and stir until it has dissolved. Pour the mixture through a fine-mesh sieve into a measuring cup or other vessel with a spout. Carefully pour the mixture into a silicone ice tray, dividing evenly among 4 large cubes. Transfer to the refrigerator and chill for at least 3 to 4 hours until solid but still jiggly.

To serve, submerge the bottom of the ice tray in a bowl of hot water for 10 seconds. Carefully remove each panna cotta cube from the ice tray and transfer to a plate. Serve with berries or a drizzle of honey.

Salted Caramel Panna Cotta

Maybe you've seen salted caramel in your favorite ice cream or candy bar. Fortunately, it's quite easy to make at home and it serves as a delicious flavoring for this panna cotta. It's important to start your caramel in a medium saucepan because as you pour the half-and-half or cream into it, the caramel will bubble up, and having space for it to expand will save you from a sticky mess!

MAKES 4 LARGE CUBES

4 TABLESPOONS	COOL WATER
2½ TEASPOONS	GELATIN
2 CUPS	HALF-AND-HALF (OR 1 CUP WHOLE MILK AND 1 CUP HEAVY CREAM)
½ TEASPOON	VANILLA EXTRACT
½ CUP	SUGAR
¼ TEASPOON	FLAKY SEA SALT, FOR GARNISH
	CARAMEL POPCORN, FOR GARNISH (OPTIONAL)

In a small bowl, combine 3 tablespoons of water and gelatin. Set aside.

Meanwhile, in a measuring cup, combine the half-and-half and vanilla and set aside.

In a medium saucepan, combine the sugar and the remaining 1 tablespoon of water. Heat over medium heat and refrain from stirring. The sugar will start to melt, and as it does, swirl the pan to distribute any unmelted sugar. Once the sugar has melted, let it cook until it turns a deep amber color, about 2 to 3 minutes. Turn off the heat. This your caramel.

Little by little (it will sputter) whisk the cream mixture into the caramel. The caramel will harden, but don't worry and keep whisking until all the caramel has dissolved. If the caramel is not melting into the cream, turn the heat back on low. Once all the cream has been incorporated, add the bloomed gelatin and stir until it has dissolved.

Pour the mixture through a fine-mesh sieve into a measuring cup or other vessel with a spout. Carefully pour the mixture into a silicone ice tray, dividing evenly among 4 large cubes. Transfer to the refrigerator and chill for at least 3 to 4 hours until solid but still jiggly.

To serve, submerge the bottom of the ice tray in a bowl of hot water for 10 seconds. Carefully remove each panna cotta cube from the ice tray and transfer to a plate. Garnish with flaky sea salt and caramel popcorn (if using).

Green Tea Panna Cotta

Matcha desserts are all over Pinterest, and for good reason. The beautiful bright green color of this panna cotta is followed up with a punch of flavor that works great with fruit. This is also a sweet way to introduce the flavor of matcha to kids.

MAKES 4 LARGE CUBES

3 TABLESPOONS	COOL WATER
2½ TEASPOONS	GELATIN
2 CUPS	HALF-AND-HALF (OR 1 CUP WHOLE MILK AND 1 CUP HEAVY CREAM)
2 TEASPOONS	MATCHA
¼ TEASPOON	VANILLA EXTRACT
⅓ CUP	SUGAR
	STRAWBERRIES OR RASPBERRIES, FOR SERVING

In a small bowl, combine the water and gelatin. Set aside.

Meanwhile, in a small saucepan, combine the half-and-half, matcha, vanilla, and sugar. Bring to a boil, turn off the heat. Add the bloomed gelatin and stir until it has dissolved. Pour the mixture through a fine-mesh sieve into a measuring cup or other vessel with a spout.

Carefully pour the mixture into a silicone ice tray, dividing evenly among 4 large cubes. Transfer to the refrigerator and chill for at least 3 to 4 hours until solid but still jiggly.

To serve, submerge the bottom of the ice tray in a bowl of hot water for 10 seconds. Carefully remove each panna cotta cube from the ice tray and transfer to a plate. Serve with strawberries or raspberries.

Coconut and Passion Fruit Panna Cotta

Although this is the most involved of all the panna cotta in the chapter, the extra steps are well worth the effort. Serve this bright, two-layered stunner instead of a coconut and passion fruit cake.

MAKES 4 LARGE CUBES

FOR THE PASSION FRUIT LAYER:

½ TEASPOON	GELATIN
1 TABLESPOON	COOL WATER
½ CUP	PASSION FRUIT JUICE
2 TEASPOONS	SUGAR

FOR THE COCONUT LAYER:

2 TEASPOONS	GELATIN
3 TABLESPOONS	COOL WATER
1 CUP	CANNED COCONUT MILK
1 CUP	HEAVY CREAM
⅓ CUP	SUGAR

Make the passion fruit layer: In a small bowl, combine the gelatin and water. Set aside.

In a small saucepan, combine the passion fruit juice and sugar. Bring to a boil, turn down to a simmer, and cook for 5 minutes until the sugar has dissolved and some of the juice has evaporated.

Add the bloomed gelatin and stir until the gelatin has dissolved. Carefully pour the mixture into a silicone ice tray, dividing evenly among 4 large cubes. Transfer to the refrigerator and chill for 3 hours.

Make the coconut layer: In a small bowl, combine the gelatin and water. Set aside.

In a small saucepan, combine the coconut milk, heavy cream, and sugar. Bring to a simmer, stirring until the sugar has dissolved. Turn off the heat, add the bloomed gelatin, and stir until it has dissolved.

Transfer the mixture to a liquid measuring cup or other vessel with a spout. Let cool to room temperature, about 30 minutes.

Carefully pour the mixture into the ice tray on top of the passion fruit layer, dividing evenly among 4 large cubes. Transfer to the refrigerator and chill for at least 3 to 4 hours until solid but still jiggly.

To serve, submerge the bottom of the ice tray in a bowl of hot water for 10 seconds. Carefully remove each panna cotta cube from the ice tray, transfer to a plate, and serve.

Buttermilk and Honey Panna Cotta

Buttermilk adds a wonderfully tart note to this panna cotta, and—when complemented by the sweetness of the honey—produces a dessert with a mild flavor that will delight just about everyone.

MAKES 4 LARGE CUBES

1 CUP	BUTTERMILK
2½ TEASPOONS	GELATIN
1 CUP	HEAVY CREAM
⅓ CUP	HONEY, PLUS MORE FOR SERVING
½ TEASPOON	VANILLA EXTRACT
	FRESHLY GROUND BLACK PEPPER, FOR GARNISH (OPTIONAL)

In a small bowl, combine the buttermilk with the gelatin. Set aside.

Meanwhile, in a small saucepan, combine the heavy cream, honey, and vanilla. Bring to a simmer, turn off the heat.

Add the buttermilk and bloomed gelatin and stir until the gelatin has dissolved. Pour the mixture through a fine-mesh sieve into a measuring cup or other vessel with a spout.

Carefully pour the mixture into a silicone ice tray, dividing evenly among 4 large cubes. Transfer to the refrigerator and chill for at least 3 to 4 hours until solid but still jiggly.

To serve, submerge the bottom of the ice tray in a bowl of hot water for 10 seconds. Carefully remove each panna cotta cube from the ice tray and transfer to a plate. Serve with some honey and a few cracks of black pepper (if using).

Ice Cream Sandwiches

Ice cream sandwiches are the ultimate combination of the grocery store's two best treats: ice cream and cookies. They can come in any ice cream–cookie combo your heart desires, so feel free to experiment until you find your favorite. Dress up these sweet little cubes further by dipping them in crushed nuts, sprinkles, or chocolate bits—the possibilities are infinite. These treats keep up to 3 months in the freezer.

Vanilla and Graham Cracker Ice Cream Sandwiches

Using just five simple ingredients and a silicone ice tray, you can whip up a simple ice cream treat that is way greater than the sum of its parts. Roll this classic combo in colorful sprinkles to kick up the fun factor—you'll have an instant birthday party hit!

MAKES 12 SANDWICHES

6	GRAHAM CRACKERS, FINELY CRUSHED (1 CUP CRUMBS)
2 TABLESPOONS	SUGAR
4 TABLESPOONS	UNSALTED BUTTER, MELTED
1 CUP	VANILLA ICE CREAM, SOFTENED
¼ CUP	SPRINKLES, FOR GARNISH (OPTIONAL)

In a medium bowl, combine the graham cracker crumbs, sugar, and melted butter. Stir until the mixture resembles wet sand.

Spoon a heaping teaspoon of graham cracker crumbs into 12 cubes of a silicone ice tray. Using your fingers, press the crumbs down to the bottoms of the cubes, making sure it's evenly covered.

Transfer to the freezer for 5 minutes to chill.

Remove the tray from the freezer. Spoon the ice cream into each cube, dividing evenly. Using the spoon, smooth out the top, making sure there's a little space left to add the remaining graham cracker crumbs. Transfer to the freezer to chill and harden for 1 hour.

Remove from the freezer. Spoon a heaping teaspoon of the remaining crumbs on top of the ice cream in each cube. Using your fingers, gently press down on the crumbs, making sure the surface is covered evenly.

Transfer to the freezer to chill and harden for another 2 hours before popping the sandwiches out of the ice tray. To serve, place the sprinkles (if using) on a plate and roll each ice cream sandwich in them.

Vanilla and
Graham Cracker
Ice Cream
Sandwiches

Ginger and Green Tea Ice Cream Sandwiches

Green tea ice cream is now widely available in supermarkets, but if yours doesn't carry it, feel free to try other flavors. A few great options that work well with the gingersnaps are strawberry, lemon, and peach ice cream.

MAKES 12 SANDWICHES

25	SMALL GINGERSNAP COOKIES, FINELY CRUSHED (1 CUP CRUMBS)
4 TABLESPOONS	UNSALTED BUTTER OR COCONUT OIL, MELTED
1 CUP	GREEN TEA ICE CREAM, SOFTENED

In a medium bowl, combine the gingersnap crumbs and melted butter. Stir until the mixture resembles wet sand.

Spoon a heaping teaspoon of the ginger snap crumbs into 12 cubes of a silicone ice tray. Using your fingers, press the crumbs down to the bottoms of the cubes, making sure it's evenly covered. Transfer to the freezer for 5 minutes to chill.

Remove the tray from the freezer. Spoon the ice cream into each cube, dividing evenly. Using the spoon, smooth out the top, making sure there's a little space left for the remaining gingersnap crumbs. Transfer to the freezer to chill and harden for 1 hour.

Remove from the freezer. Spoon a heaping teaspoon of the remaining crumbs on top of the ice cream in each cube. Using your fingers, gently press down on the crumbs, making sure the surface is covered evenly.

Transfer to the freezer to chill and harden for at least another 2 hours before popping the sandwiches out of the ice tray and serving.

Peanut Butter and Chocolate Ice Cream Sandwiches

Out of all the treats that use peanut butter and chocolate in this book, this one might be the best and most classic recipe. To take this sandwich to the next level, mix the roasted peanuts with a bit of brown sugar and cinnamon.

MAKES 12 SANDWICHES

12	PEANUT BUTTER COOKIES, FINELY CRUSHED (1 CUP CRUMBS)
4 TABLESPOONS	UNSALTED BUTTER OR COCONUT OIL, MELTED
1 CUP	CHOCOLATE ICE CREAM, SOFTENED
½ CUP	ROASTED SALTED PEANUTS, FINELY CHOPPED

In a medium bowl, combine the peanut butter cookie crumbs and melted butter. Stir until the mixture resembles wet sand.

Spoon a heaping teaspoon of the crumbs into 12 cubes of a silicone ice tray. Using your fingers, press the crumbs down to the bottoms of the cubes, making sure it's evenly covered. Transfer to the freezer for 5 minutes to chill.

Spoon the ice cream into each cube, dividing evenly. Using the spoon, smooth out the top, making sure there's a little space left for the remaining cookie crumbs. Transfer to the freezer to chill and harden for 1 hour.

Remove from the freezer. Spoon a heaping teaspoon of the remaining crumbs on top of the ice cream in each cube. Using your fingers, gently press down on the crumbs, making sure the surface is covered evenly.

Transfer to the freezer to chill and harden for at least another 2 hours before popping the sandwiches out of the ice tray. To serve, place the peanuts on a plate and roll each ice cream sandwich in them.

Banana Pudding Ice Cream Sandwiches

Banana pudding, the Southern classic, becomes an ice cream sandwich using bananas, creamy vanilla ice cream, and a vintage vanilla wafer crust. You can make your own vanilla wafers, but it's not a real banana pudding unless you use the processed, store-bought version.

MAKES 12 SANDWICHES

20	VANILLA WAFER COOKIES, FINELY CRUSHED (1 CUP CRUMBS)
4 TABLESPOONS	UNSALTED BUTTER, MELTED
1	BANANA, SLICED INTO 12 ROUNDS
1 CUP	VANILLA ICE CREAM, SOFTENED

In a medium bowl, combine the vanilla wafer crumbs and melted butter. Stir until the mixture resembles wet sand.

Spoon a heaping teaspoon of the crumbs into 12 cubes of a silicone ice tray. Using your fingers, press the crumbs down to the bottoms of the cubes, making sure it's evenly covered. Transfer to the freezer for 5 minutes to chill.

Remove the tray from the freezer. Place a banana slice in each of the cubes. Spoon the ice cream into each cube, dividing evenly. Using the spoon, smooth out the top, making sure there's a little space left for the remaining vanilla wafer crumbs. Transfer to the freezer to chill and harden for 1 hour.

Remove from the freezer. Spoon a heaping teaspoon of the remaining crumbs on top of the ice cream in each cube. Using your fingers, gently press down on the crumbs, making sure the surface is covered evenly.

Transfer to the freezer to chill and harden for at least another 2 hours before popping the sandwiches out of the ice tray and serving.

Chocolate and Pistachio Ice Cream Sandwiches

The chocolate wafers that you might use in an icebox cake are ground up and turned into the perfect base for this ice cream sandwich. The quick roll in chopped pistachios at the end adds a satisfying crunch to the treat, so don't skip it!

MAKES 12 SANDWICHES

20	CHOCOLATE WAFER COOKIES, FINELY CRUSHED (1 CUP CRUMBS)
4 TABLESPOONS	UNSALTED BUTTER OR COCONUT OIL, MELTED
1 CUP	VANILLA OR PISTACHIO ICE CREAM, SOFTENED
½ CUP	PISTACHIOS, FINELY CHOPPED

In a medium bowl, combine the chocolate wafer crumbs and melted butter. Stir until the mixture resembles wet sand.

Spoon a heaping teaspoon of the crumbs into 12 cubes of a silicone ice tray. Using your fingers, press the crumbs down to the bottoms of the cubes, making sure it's evenly covered. Transfer to the freezer for 5 minutes to chill.

Remove the tray from the freezer. Spoon the ice cream into each cube, dividing evenly. Using the spoon, smooth out the top, making sure there's a little space left for the remaining chocolate wafer crumbs. Transfer to the freezer to chill and harden for 1 hour.

Remove from the freezer. Spoon a heaping teaspoon of the remaining crumbs on top of the ice cream in each cube. Using your fingers, gently press down on the crumbs, making sure the surface is covered evenly.

Transfer to the freezer to chill and harden for at least another 2 hours before popping the sandwiches out of the ice tray. To serve, place the pistachios on a plate and roll each ice cream sandwich in them.

Crispy Rice Treats

We've all made crispy rice treats—they are one of the greatest and simplest no-bake desserts out there. Because they traditionally come in square shapes, a silicone ice tray is the perfectly shaped mold for making them. The recipes in this chapter represent a more grownup take on crispy rice treats, with flavor combos like tahini and sea salt, and raspberry and almond. So don't be shy, bring these to your company's Christmas cookie swap. Store them well wrapped at room temperature for a few days or extend their shelf life in the refrigerator.

Jelly Doughnut Crispy Rice Treats

This treat packs all the same dreamy flavors of a jelly doughnut into a crispy rice treat. Dressed up with strawberry jam and sprinkles, this treat is a less glutinous (but equally delicious) way to satisfy your sweet tooth.

MAKES 12 TREATS

1½ CUPS	CRISPY RICE CEREAL
2 TABLESPOONS	UNSALTED BUTTER
2 CUPS	MARSHMALLOWS (ABOUT 12 PIECES)
¼ TEASPOON	VANILLA EXTRACT
¼ TEASPOON	KOSHER SALT
1½ CUPS	STRAWBERRY JAM
¼ CUP	SPRINKLES

Place the rice cereal in a large bowl and set aside.

In a small saucepan, melt the butter. Once it has melted, add the marshmallows, vanilla, and salt. Heat over low heat, stirring constantly, until everything has melted and is well combined.

Using a rubber spatula, add the mixture to the rice cereal and stir until well combined.

Spoon half of the crispy rice mixture into a silicone ice tray, dividing evenly among 12 cubes. Spoon the strawberry jam on top of the crispy rice layer in each cube, distributing evenly.

Top each cube with the remaining crispy rice mixture followed by a few sprinkles. Transfer the ice tray to the refrigerator and chill completely or until ready to serve.

Peanut Butter and Chocolate Crispy Rice Treats

Chocolate forms a base for this crispy rice treat laden with peanut butter. It's like an energy bar and dessert in one, suitable for crispy rice treat lovers big and small. Subbing in another kind of nut butter, especially almond butter, makes for a great variation.

MAKES 12 TREATS

3 OUNCES	DARK CHOCOLATE, CHOPPED, OR ½ CUP DARK CHOCOLATE CHIPS
3 TABLESPOONS	UNSALTED BUTTER
1½ CUPS	CRISPY RICE CEREAL
2 CUPS	MARSHMALLOWS (ABOUT 12 PIECES)
¼ CUP	PEANUT BUTTER
¼ TEASPOON	VANILLA EXTRACT
¼ TEASPOON	KOSHER SALT

In a heatproof bowl, combine the chocolate with 1 tablespoon of butter. Place the bowl over a small pot of simmering water, making sure the bottom of the bowl does not touch the water. Melt the chocolate, stirring occasionally. Remove from the heat. Alternatively, you can microwave the chocolate and butter in 10-second intervals, stirring in between, until melted.

Spoon the melted chocolate into a silicone ice tray, dividing evenly among 12 cubes. Transfer to the freezer immediately and chill for 10 minutes.

Meanwhile, place the rice cereal in a large bowl and set aside.

In a small saucepan, melt the remaining 2 tablespoons of butter. Once it has melted, add the marshmallows, peanut butter, vanilla, and salt. Heat over low heat, stirring constantly, until everything has melted and is well combined.

Using a rubber spatula, add the mixture to the rice cereal and stir until well combined.

Spoon the mixture into the ice tray, dividing evenly among 12 cubes. Transfer the ice tray to the refrigerator and chill completely until ready to serve.

Tahini and Sea Salt Crispy Rice Treats

Besides working very well in chocolate (Tahini Swirl Chocolates, page 20), tahini blends beautifully with marshmallows and butter to make an extra creamy crispy rice treat. Toasting the sesame seeds and using high-quality flaky sea salt are pro tips that are well worth it.

MAKES 12 TREATS

2 CUPS	CRISPY RICE CEREAL
2 TABLESPOONS	UNSALTED BUTTER
2 CUPS	MARSHMALLOWS (ABOUT 12 PIECES)
¼ CUP	TAHINI
¼ TEASPOON	VANILLA EXTRACT
⅛ TEASPOON	GROUND CARDAMOM
¼ TEASPOON	FLAKY SEA SALT
1 TABLESPOON	TOASTED SESAME SEEDS

Place the rice cereal in a large bowl and set aside.

In a small saucepan, melt the butter, then add the marshmallows, tahini, vanilla, and cardamom. Heat over low heat, stirring constantly, until everything has melted and is well combined.

Using a rubber spatula, add the mixture to the rice cereal, sprinkle in the sea salt and sesame seeds, and stir until well combined.

Spoon the mixture into a silicone ice tray, dividing evenly among 12 cubes. Transfer the ice tray to the refrigerator and chill completely until ready to serve.

Raspberry and Almond Crispy Rice Treats

Believe it or not, freeze-dried raspberries work better than fresh ones in this recipe. Crushing the freeze-dried raspberries into a superfine dust by quickly pulsing them in a food processor will help disperse the raspberry flavor throughout the treats. Almond extract is an update to this classic treat.

MAKES 12 TREATS

1½ CUPS	CRISPY RICE CEREAL
½ CUP	FREEZE-DRIED RASPBERRIES, CRUSHED
2 TABLESPOONS	UNSALTED BUTTER
2 CUPS	MARSHMALLOWS (ABOUT 12 PIECES)
¼ TEASPOON	ALMOND EXTRACT
¼ TEASPOON	KOSHER SALT

In a large bowl, combine the rice cereal and crushed freeze-dried raspberries and set aside.

In a small saucepan, melt the butter, then add the marshmallows, almond extract, and salt. Heat over low heat, stirring constantly, until everything has melted and is well combined.

Using a rubber spatula, add the mixture to the rice cereal and stir until well combined.

Spoon the mixture into a silicone ice tray, dividing evenly among 12 cubes. Transfer the ice tray to the refrigerator and chill completely until ready to serve.

Raspberry and Almond Crispy Rice Treats

NOTE: PAGE REFERENCES IN *ITALICS* INDICATE PHOTOGRAPHS.

A

Almond Butter and Chocolate Swirl Froyo Pops, 44
Arnold Palmer Jelly, 31

Banana Pudding Ice Cream Sandwiches, 79
Berries
- Breakfast Parfait Pops, 41, *43*
- Goat Cheese and Blueberry Cheesecake, 60, *61*
- Peach Raspberry Ice Pops, 50, *51*
- Raspberry and Almond Crispy Rice Treats, 87, *88*
- Strawberry Jelly, 37, *38*
- Strawberry Jelly Doughnut Crispy Rice Treats, 83
- Vanilla and Raspberry Cheesecake, 58, *59*

Blueberry and Goat Cheese Cheesecake, 60, *61*
Breakfast Parfait Pops, 41, *43*
Buttermilk and Honey Panna Cotta, 70, *71*

C

Caramel, Salted, Panna Cotta, 66, *67*
Chai Tea Coconut Ice Pops, 52
Cheese
- Goat, and Blueberry Cheesecake, 60, *61*
- Mango and Ginger Cheesecake, 57
- Mocha Cheesecake, 62, *63*
- Vanilla and Raspberry Cheesecake, 58, *59*

Cheesecakes
- Goat Cheese and Blueberry, 60, *61*
- Mango and Ginger, 57
- Mocha, 62, *63*
- Vanilla and Raspberry, 58, *59*

Chocolate. *See also* Chocolates
- and Almond Butter Swirl Froyo Pops, 44
- Coconut Truffles, 25
- Mocha Cheesecake, 62, *63*
- Peanut Butter, and Pretzel Truffles, 28, *29*
- and Peanut Butter Crispy Rice Treats, 84, *85*
- and Peanut Butter Ice Cream Sandwiches, 78
- Peppermint Truffles, *26*, 27
- and Pistachio Ice Cream Sandwiches, 80, *81*

Chocolates
- Fruit and Nut, 18, *19*
- Orange and Hazelnut, 21
- Spiced Mexican, 17
- Tahini Swirl, *19*, 20

White, with Macadamia Nuts and Coconut, 22, *23*
Cinnamon
Maple and Spice Froyo Pops, 45
Spiced Mexican Chocolates, 17
Vietnamese Coffee Ice Pops, 49
Coconut
Chai Tea Ice Pops, 52
Chocolate Truffles, 25
and Macadamia Nuts, White Chocolates with, 22, *23*
and Passion Fruit Panna Cotta, 69
Piña Colada Jelly, 34, *35*
Coffee
Iced, Cubes, 11, *14*
Mocha Cheesecake, 62, *63*
Vietnamese, Ice Pops, 49
Creamsicle Jelly, 36
Crispy Rice Treats
Jelly Doughnut, 83
Peanut Butter and Chocolate, 84, *85*
Raspberry and Almond, 87, *88*
Tahini and Sea Salt, 86

F

Froyo Pops
Breakfast Parfait Pops, 41, *43*
Chocolate and Almond Butter Swirl, 44
Mango Lassi, 46, *47*
Maple and Spice, 45
Fruit. *See also* Berries; *specific fruits*
and Nut Chocolates, 18, *19*

G

Ginger
and Green Tea Ice Cream Sandwiches, 76, *77*
and Mango Cheesecake, 57
Maple and Spice Froyo Pops, 45
Graham Cracker(s)
Key Lime Pie Ice Pops, 53, *54*
Vanilla and Raspberry Cheesecake, 58, *59*
and Vanilla Ice Cream Sandwiches, 73, *74*
Granola, in Breakfast Parfait Pops, 41, *43*
Grapefruit and Rosemary Jelly, 32, *33*
Green Tea
and Ginger Ice Cream Sandwiches, 76, *77*
Matcha Latte Cubes, 11, *14*
Panna Cotta, 68

H

Hazelnut and Orange Chocolates, 21
Honey and Buttermilk Panna Cotta, 70, *71*

I

Ice Cream Sandwiches
Banana Pudding, 79
Chocolate and Pistachio, 80, *81*

Ginger and Green Tea, 76, *77*
Peanut Butter and Chocolate, 78
Vanilla and Graham Cracker, 73, *74*
Ice Cubes
Iced Coffee, 11, *14*
Lemon, 13, *14*
Matcha Latte, 11, *14*
Mint, 13, *15*
Ice Pops
Coconut Chai Tea, 52
Key Lime Pie, 53, *54*
Peach Raspberry, 50, *51*
Vietnamese Coffee, 49

J

Jellies
Arnold Palmer Jelly, 31
Creamsicle Jelly, 36
Grapefruit and Rosemary Jelly, *32*, 33
Piña Colada Jelly, 34, *35*
Strawberry Jelly, 37, *38*
Jelly Doughnut Crispy Rice Treats, 83

K

Key Lime Pie Ice Pops, 53, *54*

L

Lemon
Arnold Palmer Jelly, 31
Ice Cubes, 13, *14*
Lime, Key, Pie Ice Pops, 53, *54*

M

Macadamia Nuts and Coconut, White Chocolates with, 22, *23*
Mango
and Ginger Cheesecake, 57
Lassi Froyo Pops, 46, *47*
Maple and Spice Froyo Pops, 45
Marshmallows
Jelly Doughnut Crispy Rice Treats, 83
Peanut Butter and Chocolate Crispy Rice Treats, 84, *85*
Raspberry and Almond Crispy Rice Treats, 87, *88*
Tahini and Sea Salt Crispy Rice Treats, 86
Matcha
Green Tea Panna Cotta, 68
Latte Cubes, 11, *14*
Mexican Chocolates, Spiced, 17
Mint
Chocolate Peppermint Truffles, *26*, 27
Ice Cubes, 13, *15*
Mocha Cheesecake, 62, *63*

N

Nut(s)
Chocolate and Pistachio Ice Cream Sandwiches, 80, *81*
and Fruit Chocolates, 18, *19*

Macadamia, and Coconut, White Chocolates with, 22, *23*
Orange and Hazelnut Chocolates, 21
Peanut Butter and Chocolate Ice Cream Sandwiches, 78
Spiced Mexican Chocolates, 17

O

Orange
Creamsicle Jelly, 36
and Hazelnut Chocolates, 21

P

Panna Cotta
Buttermilk and Honey, 70, *71*
Coconut and Passion Fruit, 69
Green Tea, 68
Salted Caramel, 66, *67*
Vanilla, 65
Passion Fruit and Coconut Panna Cotta, 69
Peach Raspberry Ice Pops, 50, *51*
Peanut Butter
Chocolate, and Pretzel Truffles, 28, *29*
and Chocolate Crispy Rice Treats, 84, *85*
and Chocolate Ice Cream Sandwiches, 78
Peanuts
Peanut Butter and Chocolate Ice Cream Sandwiches, 78
Spiced Mexican Chocolates, 17
Peppermint Chocolate Truffles, *26*, 27
Pineapple, in Piña Colada Jelly, 34, *35*
Pistachio(s)
and Chocolate Ice Cream Sandwiches, 80, *81*
Fruit and Nut Chocolates, 18, *19*
Pretzel, Chocolate, and Peanut Butter Truffles, 28, *29*

R

Raspberry
and Almond Crispy Rice Treats, *87*, *88*
Peach Ice Pops, 50, *51*
and Vanilla Cheesecake, 58, *59*
Rosemary and Grapefruit Jelly, *32*, 33

S

Salted Caramel Panna Cotta, 66, *67*
Sesame seeds
Tahini and Sea Salt Crispy Rice Treats, 86
Tahini Swirl Chocolates, *19*, 20
Spice and Maple Froyo Pops, 45
Spiced Mexican Chocolates, 17
Strawberry
Jelly, 37, *38*
Jelly Doughnut Crispy Rice Treats, 83

T

Tahini
- and Sea Salt Crispy Rice Treats, 86
- Swirl Chocolates, *19*, 20

Tea
- Arnold Palmer Jelly, 31
- Chai, Coconut Ice Pops, 52
- Green, and Ginger Ice Cream Sandwiches, 76, *77*
- Green, Panna Cotta, 68
- Matcha Latte Cubes, 11, *14*

Truffles
- Chocolate, Peanut Butter, and Pretzel, 28, *29*
- Chocolate Coconut, 25
- Chocolate Peppermint, *26*, 27

V

Vanilla
- and Graham Cracker Ice Cream Sandwiches, 73, *74*
- Panna Cotta, 65
- and Raspberry Cheesecake, 58, *59*

Vietnamese Coffee Ice Pops, 49

W

White Chocolates with Macadamia Nuts and Coconut, 22, *23*

Y

Yogurt
- Breakfast Parfait Pops, 41, *43*
- Chocolate and Almond Butter Swirl Froyo Pops, 44
- Mango Lassi Froyo Pops, 46, *47*
- Maple and Spice Froyo Pops, 45